BUSINESS BLUNDERS!

10 DANGEROUS BUSINESS MISTAKES

And How to Protect Your Business So It Can Thrive!

R. SHAWN MCBRIDE

Managing Member, The R. Shawn McBride Law Firm, PLLC
and Chief Innovation Officer, McBride For Business, LLC

Business Blunders!
10 Dangerous Business Mistakes and How to Protect Your Business so It Can Thrive!

R. Shawn McBride, CPA, Esq.

Published by:
McBride For Business, LLC
www.mcbrideforbusiness.com

ISBN: 978-0692733073

Disclaimer: The information and ideas presented in this book are for educational purposes only. No attorney-client relationship is formed by the use of this book, and this book does not constitute legal advice. This book is not intended to be a substitute for consulting with a qualified attorney. You should consult an attorney of your choice to discuss and implement your particular legal strategies. The author and publisher disclaim any liability arising directly or indirectly from this book.

PRAISE FOR BUSINESS BLUNDERS

"I highly recommend this book for anyone who currently owns or plans to start a business. Many business owners get so excited about the way things are today that they forget to plan for future events and the fact is, circumstances and people change over time, which can have a dramatic impact on a business and its owner. This book gives clear, compelling, and relevant advice to protect any business and prepare for sustainable and profitable growth for today and the journey to the future."

– Tom Allen
CEO, *Opango.com*

"R. Shawn McBride has written a prescription for any small business owner that will not only build their immunity against any seen or unseen vulnerability, but also shows companies how to arm themselves with indispensable strengths that can fortify a business to succeed and prosper. This book is loaded with steps that are very simple and easy to read and apply. Read it and REAP!"

– Joe Yazbeck
President, Prestige Leadership Advisors
Bestselling author of *No Fear Speaking*
International speaker and coach

"I recommend this book to business owners as well as any entrepreneur who's ever dreamed about having a business. And as a journalist who took a graduate course in business reporting, I'd also recommend this book to anyone who covers companies. It's a quick, easy-to-read education on how to start and protect a business. The Success Checklists are brilliant and helpful. Shawn McBride is a business advisor who cares about the success of others."

– Lorri Allen
Journalist

"This is a must-read for business owners! A book to keep handy, read often, and follow its advice! Thank you!"

– Darren Bowen
CEO, Legacy Restorations, Inc.

"Shawn, thank you for writing this book. It has become a road map for my business. I have already shared this book with many of my clients and suppliers. Great job!

– Betty Garrett
CMP, President, Garrett Speakers International, Inc.

"This book is the equivalent of an insurance policy against business failure. Great advice and a valuable read. Well done!"

– Anne Bruce
Bestselling author of more than 20 books for McGraw-Hill Publishing
Speaker and executive coach

FOREWORD

Shawn McBride's book, *Business Blunders*, provides businesses with an extraordinary amount of high-level, actionable information to help make a business successful and protect it from unforeseen or unplanned situations.

Karl Sagan once said, *"What an astonishing thing a book is. It's a flat object made from a tree with flexible parts on which are imprinted lots of funny dark squiggles. But one glance at it and you're inside the mind of another person, maybe somebody dead for thousands of years. Across the millennia, an author is speaking clearly and silently inside your head, directly to you. Writing is perhaps the greatest of human inventions, binding together people who never knew each other, citizens of distant epochs. Books break the shackles of time. A book is proof that humans are capable of working magic."* This is the case with this book as well. Climbing inside the mind of one of today's leading business minds is a good thing to do from time to time; much can be learned from McBride's experience and advice.

Anyone in business today has to deal with myriad of challenging issues whether they like it or not. The stakes have never been higher and the complexity of running a business does not appear to be lessening any time soon!

Shawn's book provides peace of mind, puts you in control, and offers key planning steps. All of these outcomes are to be welcomed if you are serious about building your business and enhancing its longevity.

There is a wealth of information contained in this quick worthwhile read, making it ideal for anyone starting a business or running one. I gained a lot from reading McBride's book and I'm sure you will too.

– Jim Whipp
President/CEO, St. Agnes Federal Credit Union

TABLE OF CONTENTS

"No, I am not your first customer. I am your first litigator. You failed to put a warning on your glass door causing my client to walk right into it. See you in court."

PREFACE

As the managing member of a boutique law firm and later a consulting firm, I am fortunate to get to see a variety of situations involving business owners. Prior to running that law firm I worked for a number of large law firms where I saw similar themes. So many years, so many recurring themes.

However, not all of these recurring themes seen in my legal practice and interaction with business owners are positive. Too much wealth is lost every day, every week, every month from little things missed by businesses.

Out of the frustration of seeing too many businesses making mistakes they often didn't even realize they were making came the inspiration for this book. I wanted a short and powerful guide that I could share with my clients and other businesses I encounter. These are things every business can assess to make sure they are on the right track.

Here you will find a practical business tool, that business owners, investors, managers, and even employees could use as a checklist—something to focus their thoughts and to make sure that small and large things are not being missed. *Business Blunders!* identifies potential problems and offers strategies to protect business, all with an eye on maximizing wealth.

HOW TO USE THIS BOOK

This is your guide to identifying and addressing common challenges and pitfalls in your business; you will want to refer to it regularly.

I recommend reading this book cover-to-cover the first week you receive it. You should also make a calendar note to review the table of contents once per quarter with your advisors. Once per year you'll want to revisit the entire book cover-to-cover to keep you on track.

INTRODUCTION

Sometimes we don't know what we don't know. The same applies in our professional lives. Fortunately mistakes from the things we don't know can often be corrected or avoided in some manner, and all mistakes provide a learning experience—for both our firm and our clients. The mistakes and failures of prior clients and those unfortunate souls called before a court to litigate over their alleged mistakes creates a safer path for future clients.

What is the root cause of most situations that cause a disruption or loss of value in a business? A lack of planning. Some will try to sugarcoat or rationalize it, but when you trace it back, typically someone just failed to plan. Most of the difficult situations clients bring to my practice are things that could have been avoided. Talk about an ounce of prevention providing a pound of cure!

You have before you a powerful book. Reviewing the lessons contained herein and doing some advance planning can and will help you avoid a number of potential problems and save you a great deal of money.

"I would like to introduce our new partner to the firm, my ex-wife Marge who owns 60% of my stock options and Max her divorce lawyer who made it all possible."

1. PLAN FOR A CHANGE IN PARTNERS/OWNERSHIP

B usiness owners believe their business partnership will last forever. Just as friends (and occasionally spouses) come and go, business partners also come and go—sometimes multiple times.

It is not uncommon for business professionals to be involved in many partnerships throughout their business lives. Many people go into business partnerships knowing that they aren't supposed to last for a lifetime. Additionally, there is very little social stigma around changing partners and people adjust to economic realities and make changes, so the possibility of a partnership dissolving is very real and planning for this is essential. Even if the partnership is envisioned to be a long-term one, unexpected events can happen and exit planning is foundational to avoid problems down the road.

Each partnership is unique and requires customized planning. However, some aspects of partnerships come up over and over again. Four areas to plan for in all partnerships are:

Death: If a partnership lasts long enough, statistical odds are 100% a partner will die.

Disability: What if one of your owners cannot contribute time, effort, or experience in the future?

Divorce: What if one of the owners splits from their spouse? Without planning that ex-spouse usually becomes part of the business and a part owner. Do you invite your new "partner" to all your meetings? What if their financial needs are not met?

Disagreement: What if the owners start to disagree? How does the business continue? In family or closely held entities this becomes important very early in the process. Who controls, who gets stock, who participates in gains, and how much pay each family member gets are just some of the issues you can anticipate.

It's very smart to sit down early and plan for the "what if" scenarios to protect the company in the event that something dissolves the partnership.

SUCCESS CHECKLIST

HOW DO I DO IT?

Step 1. Discussion: Have all of the business partners discuss their future goals for the business, including what they want from the business and how they want it to operate. This is a good time to go to a white board and/or get out some paper.

Step 2. Determine: Describe and set the limits of the business: What specifically does your business do? What doesn't it do? What activities will your business engage in? What won't it do? If you are an auto shop, do you do oil changes or repairs or both? Do you work on cars or heavy trucks or both? While some of these seem like minor details, they make a big difference in making sure business partners are on the same page about the business. Also, you will want to define where possible exit points are. (More on this in Tip 6.)

Step 3. Document: Put together the legal documents showing what the partners/co-owners have determined.

Step 4. Do it! Execute on the business in accordance with the documents, and adjust as needed!

WHEN SHOULD I DO IT?

As soon as possible. A lot of business partnerships come together and start operating without thinking about the future. Then something changes and fights ensue; in extreme cases all of the value in the company can be destroyed. That's the last thing you want to happen to your business.

TYPES OF DOCUMENTS

The types of documents needed will vary by entity and situation, but here are some possibilities:

1. **Corporation:** Certificate of incorporation, bylaws, and shareholder's agreement that all work together.
2. **LLC:** Limited liability company agreement with a detailed provision on buy/sell and management/control. Some lawyers put some provisions in member agreements or other external documents. My opinion is that it's best to put everything in one document.
3. **Partnership:** Partnership agreement with a detailed provision for buy/sell and management/control.

"As you can see, things seemed under control until August when we hired Bob our new out-of-control controller."

2. KEEP GREAT RECORDS; IT PAYS DIVIDENDS LATER

Record keeping is boring. Few people enjoy it, particularly those running businesses. But what if I told you that record keeping is key to your future wealth? And what if I told you good record keeping makes your business more powerful?

Well, it's true. Unfortunately, we often see businesses that do not keep great records. While bad records could just be a day-to-day frustration and an operational issue, a bigger issue looms: those poorly kept records might prevent a future sale of the company (or lower the company's value in an acquisition negotiation), may lead to greater liability in the event of an audit, or may hurt the company's position in the event of litigation.

The reason for poor record keeping is understandable. Often, in the startup phase, businesses are rushing to get proof of concept and to make sure the business actually works. They're not as concentrated or focused on keeping records and making sure that details are available. However, tax authorities may want to see those records. Customers or suppliers may see them at some point, depending on certain business relationships, particularly strategic long-term relationships. Additionally the records can be used to document what really happened in the event that there is litigation about an action of the company.

Importantly, if the business is ever sold the acquirer will often insist on seeing records as part of their due diligence. It's imperative that a business and its owners start keeping records from the very beginning. Document all incoming cash, outgoing payments, and payroll. Document customer lists, suppliers, and details of the agreements with those parties, including files of all contracts and agreements with all customers and suppliers. You will also want to keep records of any patents, copyrights, legal proceedings, incorporation filings and papers, etc. The more documents that are available the better. The more organized those records are the more value will be created for the business in the event of a sale, and the more protected the business will be in the event of an audit or other issue.

SUCCESS CHECKLIST

HOW DO I DO IT?

Talk to someone who has done it before. Your CPA and attorneys are a good place to start. You may also want to review this item with consultants who have operations experience. The key is to set a system early in your company's life, use that system, and revisit it so you can adjust the system from time to time as you learn what your company needs and respond to operational changes.

WHEN SHOULD I DO IT?

The sooner you start, the better. We find that most companies wait too long and then spend too much catching up on record keeping. Also, if you do not start early on you could lose an opportunity. A possible acquirer or possible strategic partner may ask to see your records, and if they aren't in order and available you may lose the deal—we have seen it happen too many times.

TYPES OF DOCUMENTS

Each segment of your operations should have its own filing system and some documents. Your counsel should be able to provide you a list. You can also subscribe to our law firm's mailing list as we often send tips on this area. Some examples:

1. **Corporate:** formation documents, company agreements, shareholder's agreements, amendments, stock certificates.

2. **Employment:** employment compliance documents, employment manuals, employee acknowledgements.
3. **Operations:** All customer agreements, all vendor agreements, leases, and asset lists.

"I sold part of my equity without a securities exemption from the SEC. What brings you here?"

3. UNDERSTAND SECURITIES OFFERINGS

Small companies don't have to think about securities laws, right? Wrong. Many businesses that are growing assume that securities offerings, the SEC, state securities regulators, and all the other complicated things relating to securities offerings are for the big boys, but the reality is most offers and sales of stock in a company—public or private—are controlled by securities laws in some way.

The purpose of securities laws is to protect investors, and the SEC and state authorities take that mission very seriously. The term "security" can be applied to many different type of investments, and almost all equity ownership of LLCs and corporations are securities under the scrutiny of the law which is enforced by the SEC, various state authorities, and the courts interpreting those laws.

Given how broad the definition of securities offerings is, it is typically the case that all sales of stock or equity in a company are regulated. Every time a security (many interests in a corporation or LLC, for instance) is offered or sold these regulations are typically triggered. Securities laws typically require that all securities offered or sold be registered unless there is an exemption from registration available. Few private companies want to go through the cost and time of doing a registration, which can be very expensive, so they are left to find an exemption for all securities offerings.

Which securities law exemption is best for a given company or a given situation is beyond the scope of this book. But most securities law exemptions are conditional, meaning that certain conditions must be met in order for the exemption to be available. So a company offering or selling securities must carefully structure the offer or sale to make sure they qualify for an exemption. If they do not, they may find they didn't qualify for an exemption and face legal liability for not registering their securities transaction.

To figure out how to structure your transaction and whether you might qualify for an exemption, a first step for business owners is to understand what a security is and whether or not the proposed sale or other transaction is even a securities offering. This is probably a time to consult counsel to find out. If it is a securities offering, you can consider what exemptions might be available to be used.

When attempting to use a securities law exemption, a company should keep great documentation of the securities offerings because in the event that the company is acquired or there is an investigation, it will be critical that these records be available. Keep great records, understand what a securities offering is, and make sure you're complying with all laws.

SUCCESS CHECKLIST

HOW DO I DO IT?

Securities laws are very complex. You'll want to involve counsel immediately and come up with a comprehensive plan before you take any actions.

WHEN SHOULD I DO IT?

Start planning for securities offerings as soon as you think you may be bringing in new owners or raising capital. The sooner you plan, the easier it will be. Some securities law exemptions are tied to certain timings and structures. So the sooner you start planning, the easier it will be.

TYPES OF DOCUMENTS

The types of documents you need will be determined by you and your counsel, based on the nature of your offering. Typically you would expect to see the following:

1. **PPM/private placement memorandum:** A document describing the company, its business, and the securities offered.
2. **Subscription agreement:** The agreement whereby investors agree to buy the securities offered. The investors also typically make certain disclosures about themselves and their financial status in these documents.
3. **Ancillary documents:** Stock certificates, escrow agreement, payment instructions, and other documents to facilitate the transaction.

"As the attorney for the Smith Company I must advise you that trademarking your name does not mean you can collect royalties from everyone named Smith."

4. PROTECT IMPORTANT INTELLECTUAL PROPERTY

Our experience is that companies usually either overvalue or undervalue their intellectual property; some will go to great lengths to protect something that hasn't even been tested yet while others don't even complete the most basic form of protection.

Part of this is economic reality. Companies often start out and then they're in a rush to get to market and they don't understand what intellectual property is or they don't take time to protect it.

Valuable intellectual property such as proprietary manufacturing processes, unique know-how, formulas, written materials, customer lists, etc., can be hiding in plain sight.

What are your unique value drivers, and how do you protect them? Patents, trademarks, and copyrights are all viable options for various types of intellectual property. You may also want to consider using trade secrets and protecting the information within the company by using contractual arrangements and giving out information on a need-to-know basis. It's important to understand early in your business what the intellectual property is and then plan to make sure that it is protected.

And with intellectual property the old saying "loose lips sink ships" holds true. Telling too much to the wrong person could lead to losing the rights over intellectual property or severely hurting its value. In many cases when dealing with a supplier, employee, or other person it will be key to get a non-disclosure agreement (NDA) to protect the intellectual property and set limits on how it can be used. Whenever any sensitive information is given out an NDA should be considered.

SUCCESS CHECKLIST

HOW DO I DO IT?

Start with this three-step process:

1. First, identify all the unique value drivers in your business. Why are people doing business with you or why will they be doing business with you?
2. Which of these unique value drivers could be protected legally? You may need to consult with intellectual property counsel.
3. Of the value drivers that can be protected, which are worth the expense?

WHEN SHOULD I DO IT?

The sooner the better. Your value drivers could be copied by competitors or you could lose rights by not protecting your intellectual property.

TYPES OF DOCUMENTS

The types of documents will vary, but could include:

1. **Trade secret documents and non-disclosure documents:** To keep others from giving away or using your intellectual property.
2. **Patent/trademark/trade name/copyright filings:** Filings made with government offices to express your intellectual property and to record your rights to it.

"Unfortunately Mr. Sloan, using a business check to buy a pair of diamond earrings for your wife puts your personal assets at risk."

5. PLUG THOSE LEAKS!

There is a common misconception in the market that once an LLC (limited liability company) or corporation is formed that the owners can rest easy and know their personal assets are safe. It is never that simple. Court cases have held owners personally liable for the debts of their businesses with great regularity. It's very important as transactions are happening and as the company is running that certain measures are taken to protect the owners from liability. Some of these steps are very simple, but very important if someone attempts to come after the owner's assets for the businesses' debt.

Some key items to address are:

Asset Records: There should be clear records of what business assets are and what personal assets are. There should be separate accounting and financial records for the business.

Separateness: The businesses should be run separate from the personal transactions of the owner(s). Both expenses and income should be separate. The more business and personal expenses are merged together, the more risk is there that the owner may be held personally liable for business debts.

Transact business as a business: Whenever dealing with third parties it needs to be crystal clear they are doing business with a business entity and not one of the owners or officers personally.

Contracts: Businesses and their owners need to understand the contracts they are entering into. In the early days of the business many contracts will require the owners' personal guarantee, exposing their own assets. As time progresses and the business grows, revisit these guarantees and remove them to protect more of the owners' personal assets.

SUCCESS CHECKLIST

HOW DO I DO IT?

Start building those firewalls and divisions between personal assets and business assets as soon as you can.

Have separate record-keeping systems between your business and personal assets and follow your system!

Make sure your company operates out of a limited liability entity and legal formalities are followed.

WHEN SHOULD I DO IT?

As with most items in this book, the sooner the better. When your business gets big enough (or scary enough) that you don't want to risk your personal assets if something goes bad in the business, its time to put these documents in place.

TYPES OF DOCUMENTS

The exact documents you will need depend on your circumstances. But here are some you possibilities:

1. **State filings:** Certificates of formation, etc. to notify others of your company's existence and limited liability status.
2. **Internal documents:** Company agreements, bylaws, shareholders agreements, etc. to show who owns what and how it works. You'll also want to include state-specific language here to maximize your liability protection.

3. **Records/files showing assets and title to the company's assets.**

"You could have avoided this with a well-written exit strategy."

6. KNOW WHERE THE EXITS ARE AND HOW YOU CAN USE THEM

B efore planes takes off airlines make sure that all passengers know where the exits are. Many business owners take flight without thinking about the exits. The day-to-day of running a business, making a product, collecting profits, increasing profitability, and keeping everything aligned takes a lot of time and attention. This can lead to the owners leaving a lot of money on the table.

We encourage business owners to consider the disposition of their company at the conception of their business so that they can have a smooth and desired exit as opposed to one that is thrust upon them with negative consequences. Some questions to consider are:

What is the goal?

Where is the business going?

How do you maximize the value of the business?

What would be the ideal time and way for you to exit?

Knowing these answers will allow the business to be planned from the back to the front. With possible avenues of exit known in advance the owner(s) can start focusing on how to make the business look good for a possible sale.

Another thing to consider is that a sale may come at an unexpected time. Just like you should know where plane exits are before taking off, you should also know what to do if it becomes necessary to exit your business sooner than expected. Ideally a business will have processes and procedures in place and will be able to run without the intervention of an owner on a day-to-day basis. Also you'll want your books and records in place and organized so you can get them to a potential buyer quickly. Many potential acquisitions have fallen apart when a business has been unable to produce proper record keeping or has shown disorganized books to a potential buyer.

SUCCESS CHECKLIST

HOW DO I DO IT?

All of the business owners should have a deep and honest discussion about how and when they might exit the business. Start by building a what-if chart showing different paths to exit.

Learning what each party expects and when they might exit can be very enlightening and lead to a greater alignment of interests. The more understanding all owners and control parties have on their future plans the better they can help each other achieve their goals.

WHEN SHOULD I DO IT?

This should be done before the business starts. Too many businesses are started with the owner, management, and control parties having different visions of what an exit will look like. At some point in the life of the company it becomes a major issue and inevitably the company has a setback. Wealth is lost fixing what should have been done in the beginning.

TYPES OF DOCUMENTS

The types of documents will vary by situation, but will often be referred to as a "buy-sell agreement." This buy-sell agreement may be embedded in other documents or may be a stand-alone document. The key is to have a way to allow owners, management, and control parties to exit at different times and on different conditions so that the company continues smoothly and no value is lost.

"Ladies and gentlemen, let me introduce our new digital gaming advisor."

7. GET ADVISORS

The right advisors can add so much value to a business. We all need team members around us, and it's never too soon to start bringing advisors in. Some will even provide advice for free.

How do advisors add so much value? Let's look at several important ways:

Outside perspective: They have different experiences and viewpoints, rounding out your thinking.

Take the pressure off: You have someone you can vent to who knows your business. They can also help with quick decisions.

Continuity: If you are called away for a business matter, are sick, or are otherwise unavailable your advisor can step in.

See high-level issues when the owners are in the weeds: They may be better able to look at the whole picture when the owner is involved in the day-to-day aspects of running the business.

Accountability: Good advisors will make you explain why you are where you are and monitor your progress.

Encourage clear thinking: Explaining (and defending) your decisions to advisors will force you to be clear about them, helping you to better understand your decisions.

Many people wrongly associate boards of directors with large companies. There are good reasons these companies want direction and advice from multiple perspectives, and smaller companies can benefit from the same idea.

Getting a board of advisors as early in the business development process as practical is highly desirable because, as mentioned above, it's critical to get outside points of view involved in the business to understand what's going on, to provide insight from their experience and expertise, and so that there's some continuation in the event that the owner faces a disability event or death. The board of advisors is a very practical way of making sure a business continues.

SUCCESS CHECKLIST

HOW DO I DO IT?

Determine who your ideal advisors are and see who is willing to serve. Be flexible and look for different types and sources of talent while also targeting those individuals you know will be most valuable to your company.

WHEN SHOULD I DO IT?

While sooner is often better, this is one area where you may be able to wait a bit longer than the other tips. The thoughts and input of advisors with different perspectives can propel your growth. However, a little maturity in the company and its operations sometimes gives the advisors more to work with.

As a general rule, any company over two years old or with more than two million dollars in revenue should have some advisors. As your operations grow you may need a more diverse set of advisors with more experience in more areas, so your collection of advisors may expand.

TYPES OF DOCUMENTS

The types of documents needed will vary with the type and formality of the advisor(s) chooses to employ. Some might include:
1. Letters/agreements regarding the scope of the advisor's service
2. Company documents spelling out the advisor's role (and legal responsibility or lack thereof)

3. Forms for presenting information about the company and its operations to advisors
4. Minutes/records of the advisor's meetings

"I feel much better now. I just purchased insurance to cover the possibility of losing my mind during a corporate take-over."

8. GET INSURANCE: COVER YOUR RISKS

Insurance is critical to cover risks in your business. As the saying goes, "You need to insure the losses you can't afford to take." The business can have a long life if properly executed and insured. This goes beyond just protecting the property of the business.

Unlikely events may happen to the business, causing disruption and financial trouble. Insurance can bridge this gap. Some businesses have been completely shut down by uninsured losses.

Proper insurance planning will go beyond just protecting the property owned by the business. What about the death of one of the owners, or disability, or just general commercial liability insurance? We covered the issue that owners of a business may change earlier in this book, however, it is an extremely rare business that has enough cash sitting around to cash out their owners in the event that one of them leaves the business due to a death or disability. Insurance can provide that liquidity and insurance companies are very suited to set up these types of "key man" life insurance policies and do so day in and day out.

The property of the business also needs sufficient coverage. And what about coverage for third parties that might be harmed? Insurance should also be considered (and likely purchased) for things like professional malpractice, auto accidents, slips and falls, injuries at the workplace, defective products, and other situations where the core activities of a business might lead to the financial losses of another party.

All of these potential liabilities should be visited with your insurance professional to make sure that adequate coverage is in place because your focus should be on the business, not on these risks or the financial problems that will occur if you're uninsured or underinsured.

SUCCESS CHECKLIST

HOW DO I DO IT?

Find a reputable insurance broker that you can trust. Explain your operations to them and look for points of risk together. Discuss available coverage options and choose the right coverage while balancing cost and benefits.

WHEN SHOULD I DO IT?

This should be done at the inception of your company. It should also be revisited at least annually and perhaps more often if operations are changing.

TYPES OF DOCUMENTS

The main documents will be insurance policies. Typical policies may include:

1. General liability
2. Property coverage
3. Malpractice (or error and omissions)
4. Directors and officers
5. Automobile

ACE BUSINESS CONSULTING

"Eighty percent of your sales coming from one customer is not a good application of the 80/20 rule, Mr. Simms."

9. DON'T PUT YOUR EGGS IN ONE CUSTOMER OR SUPPLIER BASKET

Businesses often grow in an erratic manner. Some parts of the business will grow faster than others. Every once in a while a star customer will show up and buy lots of your product or you'll find a great supplier whose products sell like wildfire.

In either situation you are likely to end up with a big problem: concentration risk, that is to say having too many eggs in one basket. The domination of your business by one supplier or one customer can have disastrous effects. An issue or disruption with that one supplier or customer could easily shut your business down, or at the very least cause uncomfortable times.

Valuation professionals know this issue well. When comparing two similar businesses, one with concentration and one without, the one without will be worth more.

In the event you that sell your business, a buyer will be unlikely to pay as much for a business that has all of its profits concentrated in one customer or supplier because the loss of that customer or supplier could be very costly to the long-term value of the business. Additionally, it gives the supplier or customer a lot of leverage. As you're building your business you need to think about diversifying your customers. Consider developing additional product offerings or other ways to make sure that you're not concentrating all of your assets and all of your risk in one customer or one supplier because it will both hurt your valuation and also create undue jeopardy for your overall business.

SUCCESS CHECKLIST

HOW DO I DO IT?

Monitor customer and vendor lists and run regular reports showing how much of your sales or expenses are with a particular customer or vendor over a period of time. Ideally you'll want to review these reports quarterly and on an annual basis. Think carefully when adding a new significant customer or vendor. While the growth of your business should be celebrated by management, you also want to understand and control the risk of taking on different types of clients or new lines of business.

WHEN SHOULD I DO IT?

Start early in your company's life and do this regularly (perhaps as part of monthly review meetings).

TYPES OF DOCUMENTS

In order to monitor this you'll want to look at the following documents:
1. Sales reports
2. Purchases reports
3. Vendor contracts

"For a limited time only, you can purchase our Extra Large Value Pack of Litigation Services for just one low price. Order today, you're going to need it."

10. PLAN FOR LITIGATION—IT'S PART OF THE GAME

Most companies will face litigation at one point or another. This is particularly true in the technology arena. Quite simply litigation is a cost of doing business.

The US (and many other Western countries) has a legal system built around litigation. It is one of the main mechanisms of accountability. Whether you agree with this system or not it's there and it's used by others.

Rightly or wrongly, someone might attempt to hold you accountable for some action at some point. And it's very likely going to cost money whether you are ultimately found to be right or wrong. There are countless clients who have faced very large legal bills defending an action that they knew was morally and legally right.

You'll want to plan for this very possible eventuality by keeping good records, understanding all levels of your business, and implementing strategies to mitigate risk.

PLANNING STEPS FOR LITIGATION:

1) Implement procedures that limit the risk of lawsuits:
What can you do to make it less likely someone will be harmed by your business?

   a. Can you make your product safer?

   b. Can you help a user understand your service better so they understand the value you are providing and won't think you short-changed them or delivered the wrong product?

   c. How are you interfacing with potential plaintiffs? Are you keeping them on your side and liking you? Do they feel like they can complain to you and get a remedy without going to court?

2) Keep good records. Many business records are admissible in litigation. So, it is worth repeating, make *sure* you are keeping good records; they will help you later.

3) Budget and prepare. Plan on litigation costs and set money aside for it.

4) Have the right staff. Having people on your team with a good attitude and that follow procedures of your company will lead to a lower number of potential lawsuits.

SUCCESS CHECKLIST

HOW DO I DO IT?

Consult with your legal team and explain your operations to them so that they can help you understand your risk points.

WHEN SHOULD I DO IT?

The sooner you start, the better. If you can manage this risk from early in the process you may avoid lawsuits. In some cases you can adjust your business model or operations to make lawsuits much less likely.

TYPES OF DOCUMENTS

The types of documents needed will vary widely by industry and the way your company operates. Good records can be key. You'll want to know what might come out in litigation and how it will look. You will also want to position your company to be in the best possible position in the event of litigation, and having proper documents and records will help you do that.

NEXT ACTION STEPS

YOU CAN START PROTECTING YOUR BUSINESS AND PREPARE IT TO THRIVE IN 3 EASY STEPS:

1. Start using this book as a checklist as suggested in the beginning of this book. Each chapter also has steps for follow.
2. Sign-up for our law firm's newsletter to get the latest news on business law: www.mcbrideattorneys.com
3. Sign-up for my consulting firm's newsletter to get updates on best business practices: www.mcbrideforbusiness.com
4. Set your plan and speak to your counsel to manage your legal risk and maximize value.

ADDITIONAL INFORMATION/ FUTURE LEARNING

R. Shawn McBride is a frequent speaker on business topics and informs lawyers, business owners, and other audiences on the legal issues involved in running a business. You can learn more about him and his speaking engagements at www.rshawnmcbridelive.com.

We also invite you to visit our websites at www.mcbrideattorneys. com and join our newsletter to get regular tips on business law and www. mcbrideforbusiness.com for business updates. On our firm's website you will also find our blog, which covers business law issues in more depth. We always enjoy suggestions of topics you would like to see, and it helps us keep a pulse on the current issues faced by business owners.

Future books discussing legal issues relevant to businesses are planned. If reading about business law issues is of interest to you please keep an eye out.

If you desire a more personal interaction to deal with your unique situation(s), do not hesitate to contact our office at 214-418-0258 for personalized consulting or to have us speak with your organization.

HAVE A STORY TO SHARE?

D o you have a business story to share? We would love to hear your experiences and ideas. Send it in, and we may feature it in a blog post, a speech, or even a future edition of this book! You can find us at www.mcbrideforbusiness.com.

ACKNOWLEDGEMENTS

I would like to acknowledge the amazing team that has assembled around me. Through the random walk of business and life I have been fortunate to have amazing minds help me at various times to allow me to gain the knowledge set forth in this book.

To my parents, Ron and Tammy McBride, thank you for setting the foundation and giving me a love of learning and encouraging me to seek more.

To my lifelong friend, Jim Whipp, thank you for always being a phone call away to discuss whatever the day's issue is.

To my team at the firm, thank you for being there and doing the great work you do to support our clients, their projects, and their goals, and for doing the research to keep us on the cutting edge of business law and doing things other firms don't do.

To the team of professional advisors that have come on board to give the push to get this book done and to accelerate my speaking career, thank you!

And thank you to those of you who are reading this book.

ABOUT R. SHAWN MCBRIDE, CPA, ESQ.

R. Shawn McBride is founder and managing member of The R. Shawn McBride Law Firm, PLLC, which concentrates on helping small to mid-size businesses protect their assets, thrive in all business situations, and ultimately reach their desired outcomes. Providing highly personalized service and educating his clients so that they understand the law and can make sound decisions on legal matters affecting their business are his highest priorities.

R. Shawn has guided the firm to be business focused, which is not surprising given his college degrees in accounting and business administration (with a concentration in finance). He passed the CPA exam prior to advising his first legal client and is currently licensed to practice law in twelve states and the District of Columbia. He is also licensed as a CPA in Maryland and Texas.

Keeping the firm true to its mission to protect business owners, R. Shawn is commonly involved in most firm client matters, whether it is looking at buy-sell arrangements for a client that owns part of a business to protect their long-term wealth, helping a company successfully bring in investors, or assisting a company in the sale of their business.

When not working on client matters, R. Shawn oversees daily operations, business development, and client management for the entire firm. R.Shawn is also an in-demand speaker about business law. For a list of topics visit www.rshawnmcbridelive.com. He also heads the Dallas office and has managerial and administrative responsibility over that location.

R. Shawn McBride is also the Chief Innovation Officer at McBride For Business, LLC. McBride For Business, LLC was formed as a response to increasing demand for Shawn's knowledge to be applied to business matters in addition to his foundation in the law.

R. Shawn's personal interests include travel, education, speaking, reading, antique cars (particularly '70s-era muscle cars including his plum-crazy 1970 Dodge Challenger convertible), museums, sports, mountains, and beaches.

Read more about R. Shawn at www.mcbrideforbusiness.com.